AZZURRA

The Dragons of Plenshia : Book One

Written by Mel Dee Dzelde
Art by Donna Sharam

ABN: 41583148542

To Contact Mel :
Facebook: https://www.facebook.com/Dragons.Plenshia
Instagram: @meldeedzelde | @dragons.plenshia

To Contact Donna:
Website: www.donnasharam.com
Facebook: www.facebook.com/DonnaSharamArt
Instagram :@donnasharamartgallery

Copyright © 2021

First Published: May 2021

The moral rights of the author have been asserted.

All rights reserved.

This book may not be reproduced in whole or in part, stored, posted on the internet or transmitted in any form or by any means, whether electronically, mechanically, or by photocopying, recording, sharing or any other means, without written permission from the author and publisher of the book. Please feel free to email me for permission – I'm usually obliging. All content found on or offline without written permission from me will be breaking the copyright law and therefore, render you liable and at risk of persecution.

ISBN: 978-0-9873024-7-2

The Dragons of Plenshia : Book One

Melody's family was BIG! She had six brothers and sisters. Everyone had a job to do to help keep their huge household running smoothly. It was Melody's job to make sure her mum's chair was pulled out and pushed in, safely seating her kind and loving mum at the table during mealtimes.

Melody's mum's chair was the prettiest at the table. It was painted green and purple with a cushion for comfort that was covered in beautiful flowers. Melody found her big wooden chair heavy today. With a grunt and a groan, she managed to complete her task. She even had enough energy left over to skip around to her chair ready for tonight's very special dinner!

She had saved as much of her energy as possible and was not going to let the cancer in her body ruin her wonderful night. She felt so excited. Maybe even too excited to eat!

The dining room was buzzing with laughter until her father's loud clapping hushed her enthusiastic siblings. He explained the rules for tonight's dinner.

"Rule number one—it is Melody's 5th birthday, so tonight, we abide by her rules.

Rule number two—it will be cake first, and spaghetti and meatballs second.

Rule number three—no singing "Happy Birthday" tonight, Melody has requested her favourite song 'Firework' from her favourite singer, Katy Perry to be her birthday song."

With that, Melody's brother Johnny, turned up the CD player and they all started singing. As they were singing, Melody's birthday cake—a multi-teared, rainbow cake with five green candles lit up the room, and every one of her loved one's faces around the table.

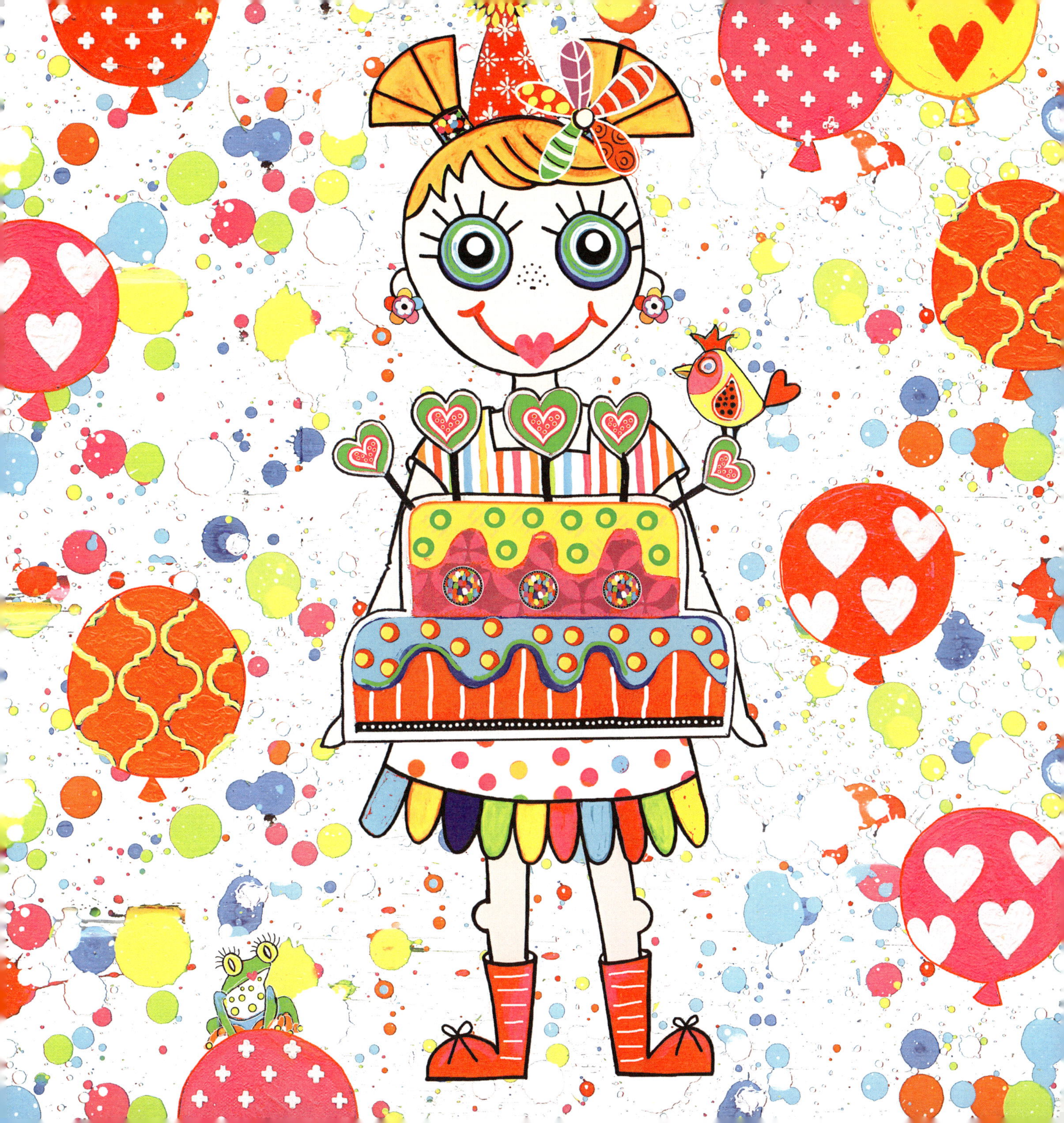

That night, as Melody lay in her warm bed, she didn't want to close her eyes. Images of her birthday played before her eyes, and she smiled as she remembered how perfect it had been. She fought to keep her eyes open, not wanting her special day to end.

It had started with her Nanny Penny joining them for breakfast. She had brought with her Melody's favourite—her famous strawberry jam and homemade loaves of bread that were still hot, and fresh from the oven. Ready to slather butter on!

Every year Melody and her siblings would be overjoyed to receive their fun musical birthday card and open it to find their treat of a twenty-dollar note inside. This year Melody's card had three dogs wearing party hats on the front. When she opened it, the dogs barked "Happy Birthday!" and it made her burst with laughter. She loved it! She adored dogs, and longed for a puppy of her own one day.

After breakfast, Melody's brothers and sister had all pitched in and made her a birthday show bag. Inside she found chocolates, marshmallows, and mixed lollies. Her mum and dad had been less strict on her having lollies lately, so Melody loved her sibling's fun and thoughtful gift.

Her mum and dad hadn't given her their present yet. Melody waited patiently. They had told her it was a gift that needed to be picked up the next morning. All she knew was it was going to be a very special gift. A gift that would help her to feel stronger. A gift that would help her to heal. "What could it possibly be?" she wondered, as her eyes got heavier and she couldn't keep them open any longer, then faded off to sleep.

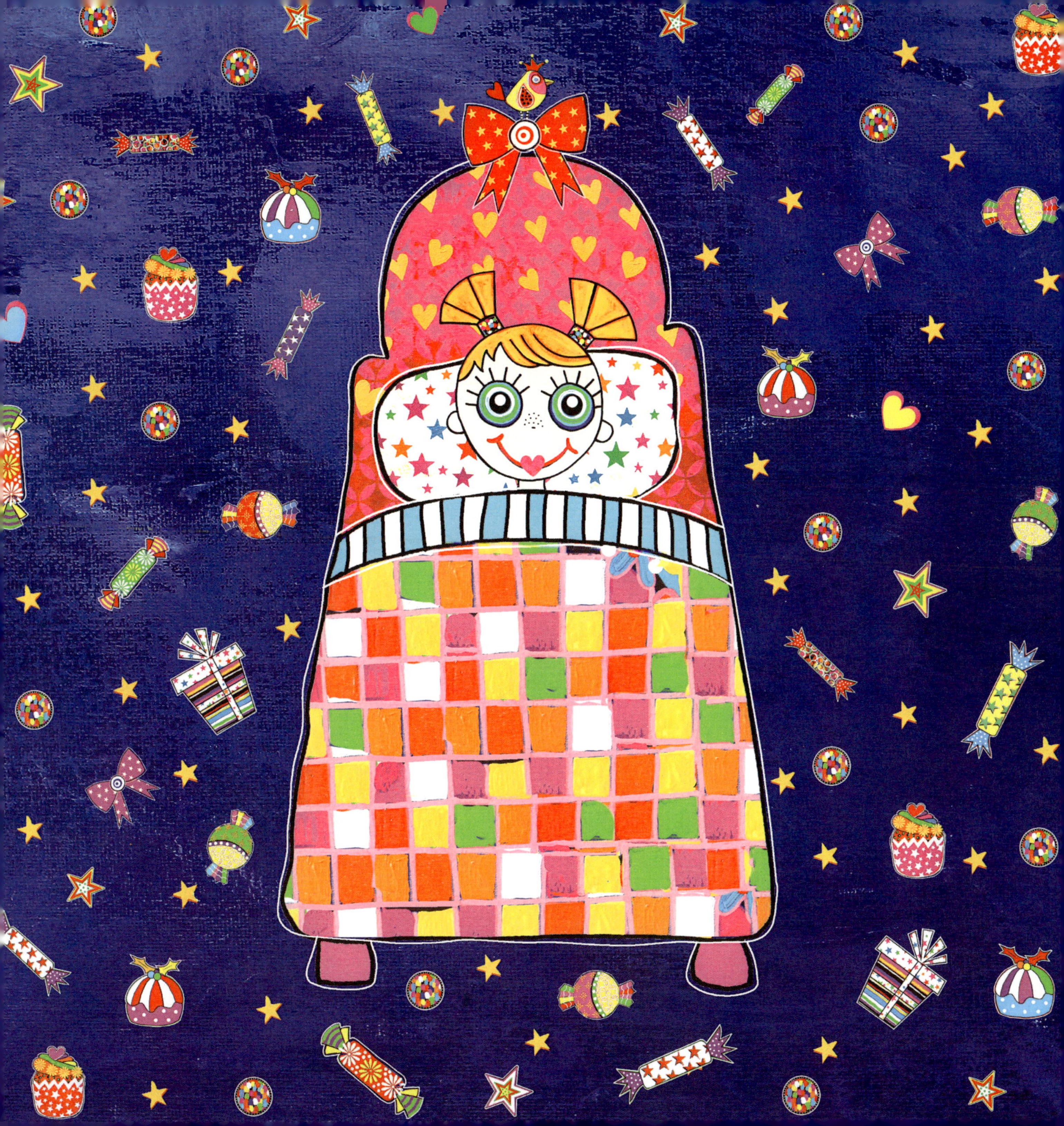

The sun beamed into Melody's room as she opened her eyes. Her orange curtains looked like they were flames dancing in the wind, as a warm breeze touched her face. Melody was alone in her room—her sister's beds were all made, and the house was quiet with her siblings already on their way to school.

The smell of strong hot coffee wafted into her room. Normally she liked it. Dad's special coffee had a chocolatey aroma about it, and he would always let her smell it straight from his steaming hot cup. Today however it made Melody's tummy feel sick.

She was having more days like this lately, and she was spending more and more time at home with her mum, going to lots of doctors who poked and prodded at her.

The cancer she had in her body meant that she'd been unwell for almost an entire year. She hardly went to kindergarten anymore, and it wasn't looking like she'd be able to start school with her best friend, Bree, which made Melody feel sad.

Just thinking about it, she let out a big, loud sigh. She didn't like being sick one bit and wished she'd been able to join her brothers, sisters and friends on the school bus that morning. A little crinkle started to appear in the middle of her forehead and hot tears welled in her green eyes. Melody tried to stop them, but they flooded her vision, pooling together in their resting place among her eyelashes before making their escape and bursting free, running down her cheeks.

Luckily her sweet mum had heard her sigh, and arrived just in time to catch her salty tears with a soft tissue, and a big warm hug.

Melody's mum always knew how to make the day brighter! She placed a pretty tray on Melody's bed topped with her daily medicine, some of Nanny Penny's strawberry jam on toast, and a glass of freshly squeezed orange juice to take away the bitter taste of medicine. Today, there was something more—a surprise! On the tray was a little red box, wrapped in a pretty green ribbon.

Another birthday gift!

"The day feels instantly better," Melody thought.

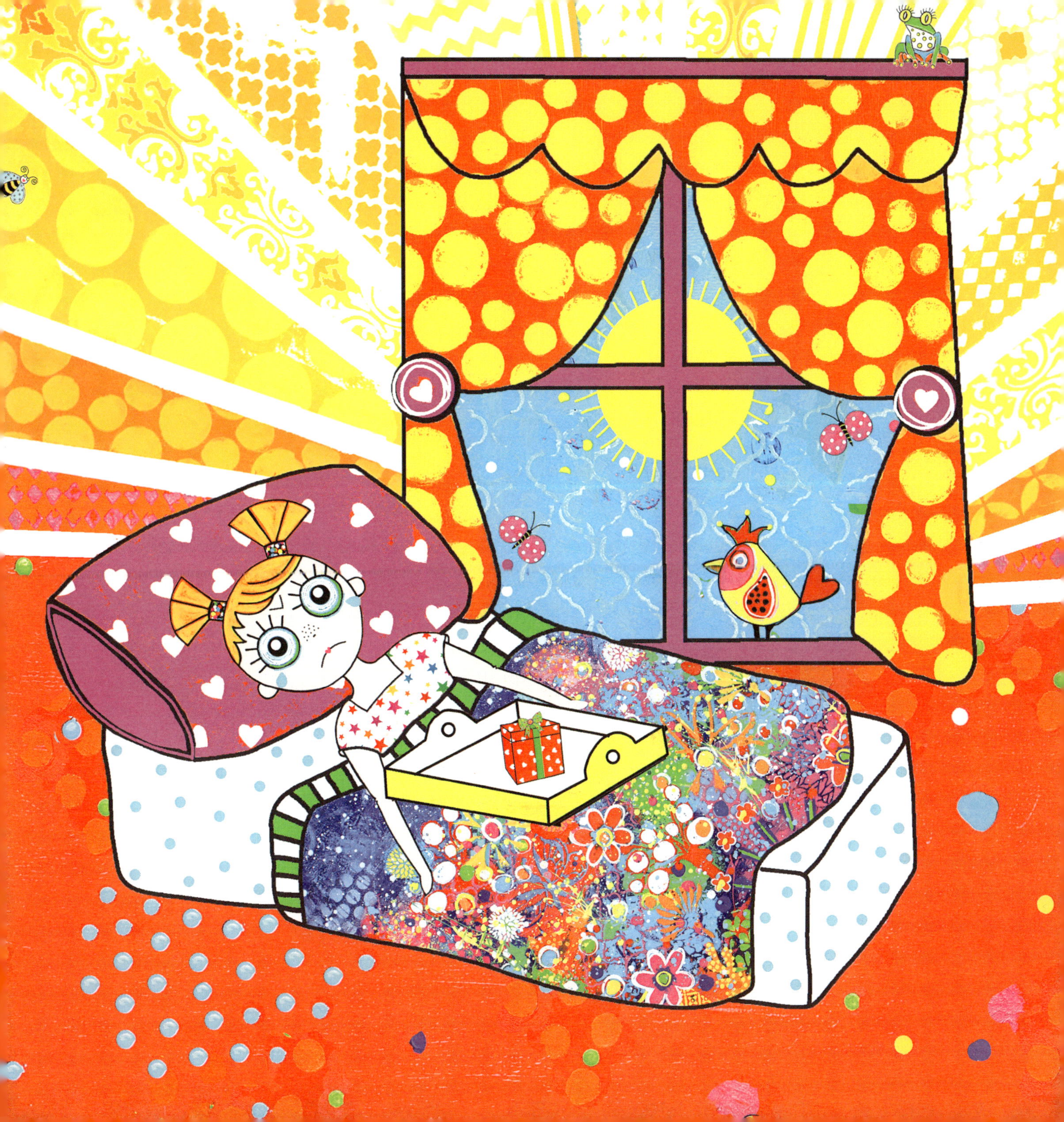

The bow on the green ribbon fell open easily as Melody pulled the knot and lifted the lid on the red box. Inside an abundance of purple tissue paper poured out, like it wanted to escape the small box quickly.

As Melody carefully peered inside, she took a quick breath. Her eyes grew wide as she found a pretty gold love heart resting in the box attached to a purple collar!

On the gold heart were some letters printed that Melody couldn't understand. Lifting her eyes to her mum, she looked at her questioningly. "Could the collar mean she was getting a dog? Or maybe a kitten?" she wondered excitedly.

The purple collar was bigger than she imagined a puppy would need, and her sister Lucy was allergic to cats, so it didn't make much sense to Melody that she would be getting either one. Her mum didn't give her much insight as she read out the name on the gold heart… "Azzurra. Your Azzurra. Now hurry up and get dressed, or we will be late!"

AZZURRA

Who was Azzurra? Or what was Azzurra?" wondered Melody on the car ride. Her mum drove into a parking space next to a tall building.

Melody stuffed her new gift in the front pocket of her new dress, a birthday gift from her Auntie Millie which she just loved, with its loud, happy colours and two big front pockets that she could put her special things into.

The gold heart name tag tinkled loudly in her pocket as Melody walked up a steep flight of stairs into what looked like another doctor's office. "Oh no!" thought Melody, she really didn't feel like going to another doctor today.

Exhausted from the stairs, her mum picked her up and gently lifted her onto a chair in the waiting room. "Azzurra is here waiting for you!" she said with a smile. Melody wanted to swing her legs with anticipation, but she felt too tired. Instead she reached inside her pocket and felt the soft felt collar.

Her tummy felt a bit better now, but it was doing something different - it felt like it was doing somersaults! Melody knew that when her tummy did that, she was feeling nervous.

Unlike some of the other doctor's waiting rooms, this one smelt like a forest. Melody could smell pine trees and wood mixed with flowers and sunshine. Large multi-coloured paintings lined the walls and bells chimed in the relaxing, gentle music that filled the air.

Suddenly a happy voice calling Melody's name interrupted her thoughts. A smiling lady wearing a dress over her pants skipped towards Melody and her mum and introduced herself as Dr. Kay. Melody couldn't stop staring—she looked completely different to all the other doctors she'd ever seen!

Dr. Kay had crazy, curly black hair, peppered with grey and purple streaks. Her bright red glasses framed her plump face and her smile filled the room with joy. Melody already loved Dr. Kay, and her outfit too! She was wearing purple shoes with her yellow and orange dress that had two big pockets on the front of it—just like Melody's!

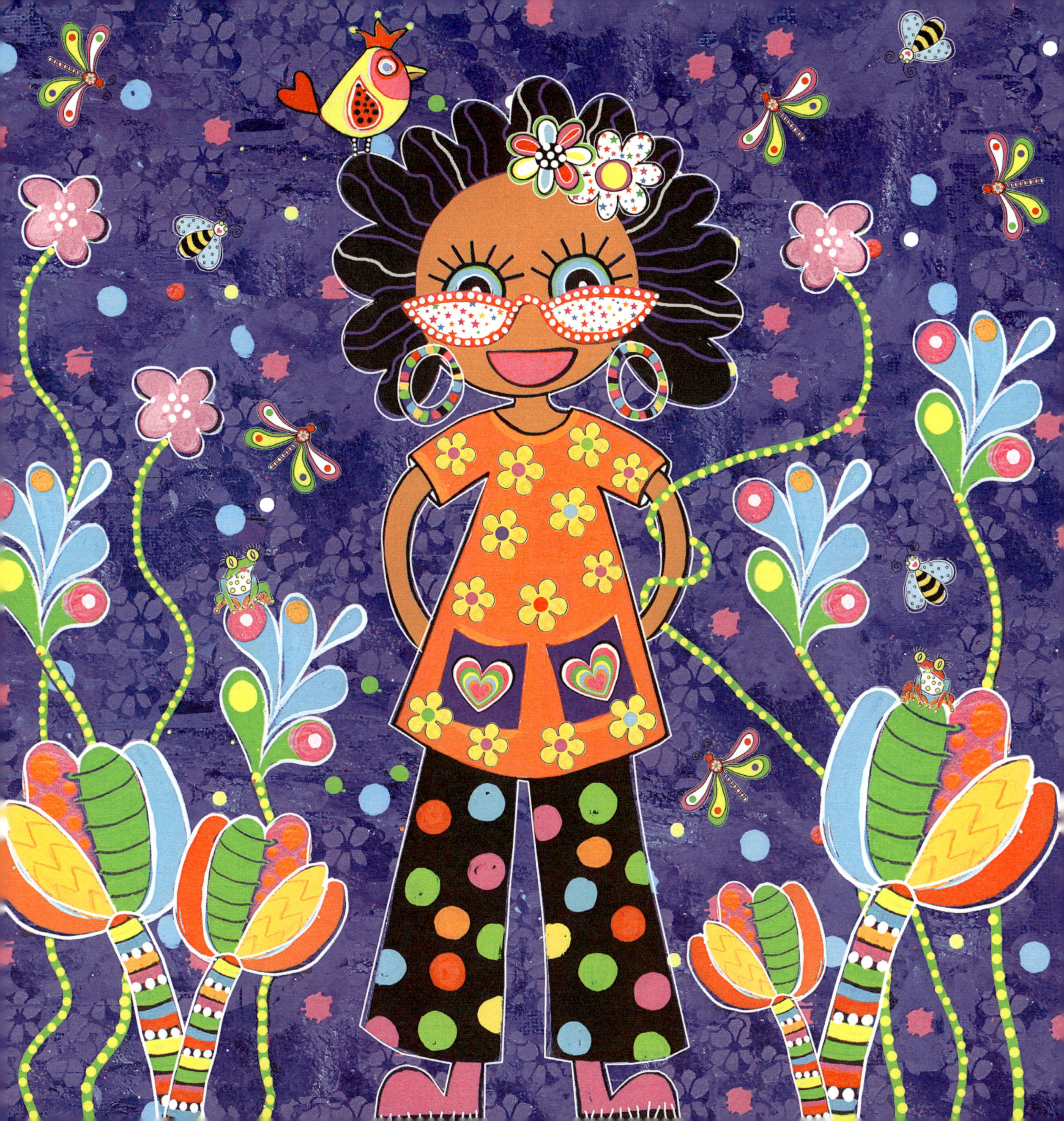

Dr. Kay asked Melody and her mum into her office which smelled like peppermint tea. Melody noticed the smell was coming from a small pot in a plume of steam, shooting up towards the ceiling like a puff of smoke. There were no puppies or kittens here, so Melody was still left wondering who her Azzurra was and when she would get to meet her. It was all so mysterious.

Dr. Kay gently held Melody's hand as she led her towards a glass case in the room which was partly covered by a red velvet cloth. Dr. Kay's happy voice became a whisper as she explained that Azzurra was only a baby now, but would grow very quickly in Melody's care, especially if she believed in magic!

Melody's eyes grew wide as Dr. Kay slowly lifted the cloth. Magic was exactly what Melody needed right now. There was a strange, mystical feeling in the room, and Melody was sure she could hear tiny fairies cheering as she finally looked inside the glass case. Her mum gasped and lifted Melody up higher for a better view.

Inside were three tiny Dragons all curled up together, fast asleep. Dr. Kay whispered "The red and black one is a boy named Luka, and the purple and black one is Asher-she was the first one to hatch. Then there's..." "Azzurra!" Melody interrupted as she quickly realised that the smallest one was hers. Her Azzurra!

Azzurra began to stir upon hearing her name. Her cream-coloured skin marked with yellow stripes shimmered under the heat lamp. "She is the plainest one there by far," thought Melody, who felt glad she had a pretty purple collar to brighten her up a little. Melody reached inside her pocket to feel the collar tinkling. Upon hearing it, Azzurra began to open her eyes.

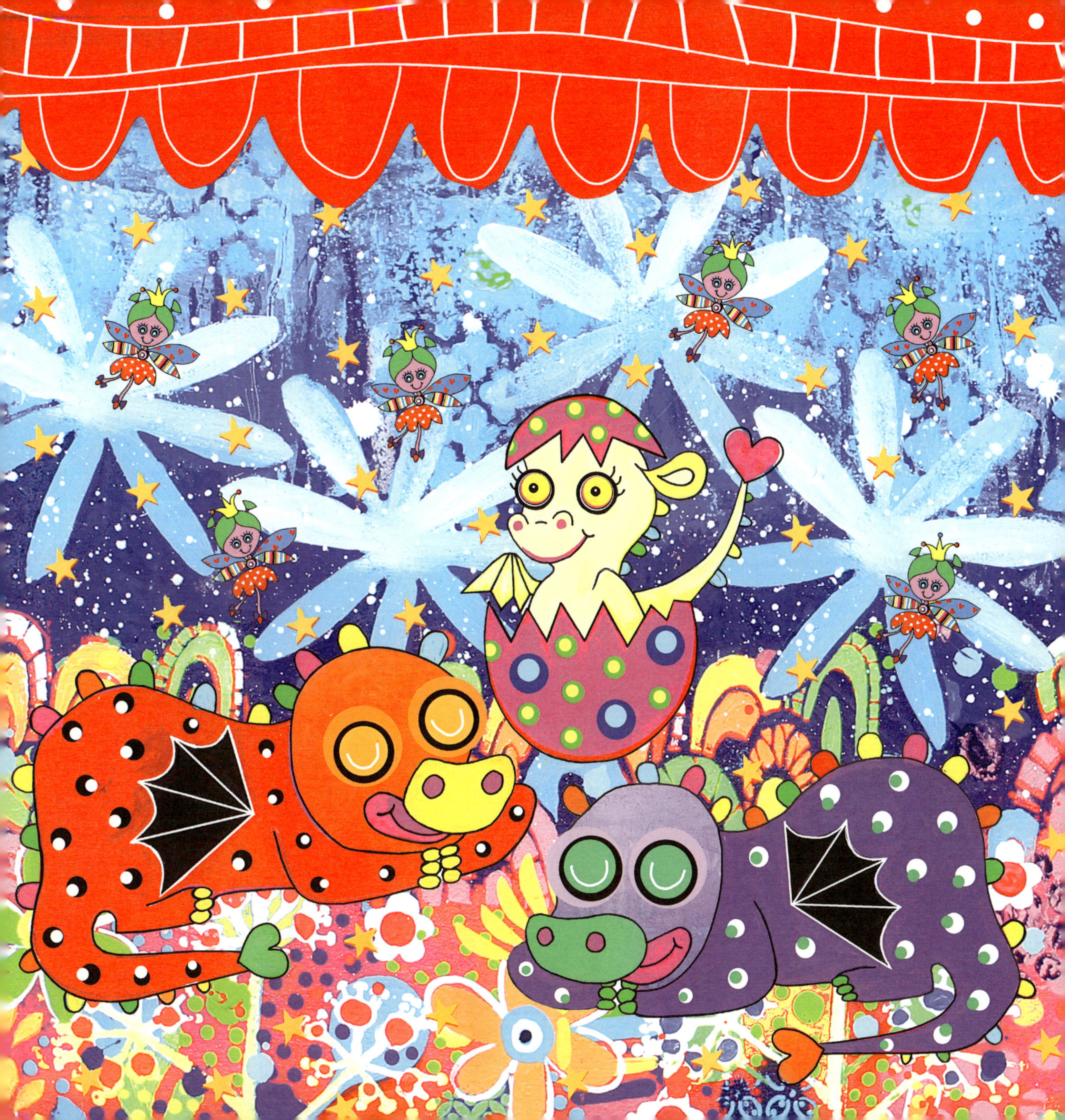

A rush of warmth filled Melody's chest as she locked eyes with her dragon for the first time. Azzurra's eyes were magical. They shimmered like a yellow sunset shining across a lake, but in all the different shades of yellow. Sparkles of mustard, sprinklings of sunshine, and flashes of daffodils shone from Azzurra like a powerful beam.

Azzurra seemed to know who Melody was and sat up reaching forward, eager to say hello. She spoke to Melody through her magical eyes. Azzurra's words floated through Melody's head as if spoken like a fairy or angel, or as if an imaginary friend was living inside her mind.

Comforting phrases like, "you are safe" and "everything is fine now" streamed from the window of Azzurra's mind into Melody's. She looked around with amazement at her mum and Dr. Kay who both had been watching on and smiling.

"Azzurra's words are only for you, Melody, and no-one else," explained Dr. Kay. She also said that Azzurra would turn a vivid green with blue and yellow stripes as she grows. Melody was delighted! Green was her favourite colour!

In that magical moment Melody felt strong and protected. The tiredness she had felt coming into the office had left her and was replaced by a mystical feeling of hope and healing. Even though she only just five years old, standing by Azzurra, she felt wise and powerful and she just knew that with Azzurra, she would somehow be cancer-free.

🌼🌼🌼

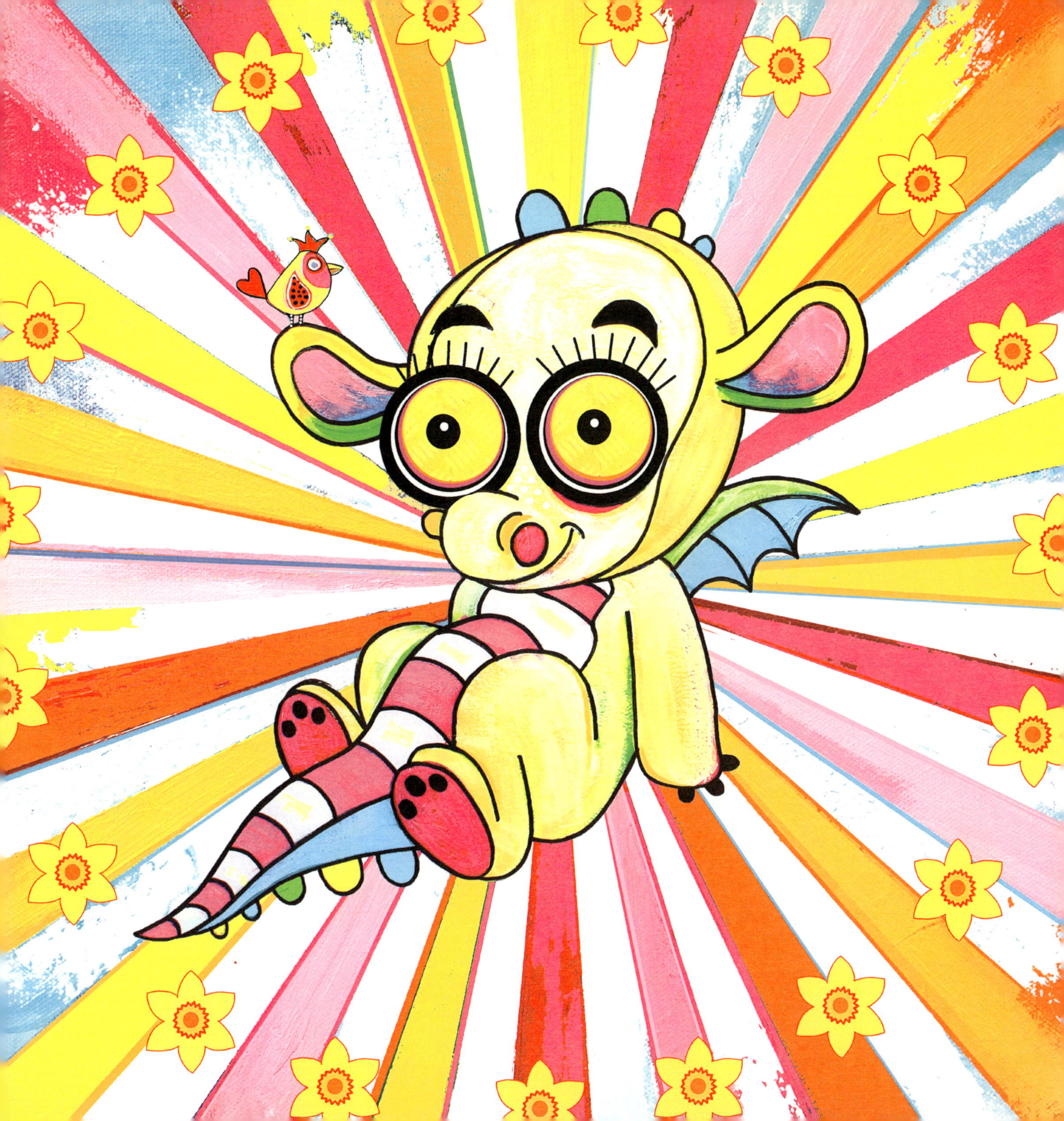

It had only been three weeks, but to Melody, it felt like she hardly knew a time before Azzurra. Their bond was greater than anything—they were happy and inseparable.

As Dr. Kay had promised, Azzurra grew quickly and started to turn a stunning vivid green, with blue and yellow stripes. Her yellow eyes became even more spectacular, if that were possible. They were big and bright and sparkled like worlds of magic. Melody adored her gorgeous little dragon.

What a big change Melody's family noticed in Melody since Azzurra had arrived. She had become more confident and faced her chemotherapy treatments without fear. She seemed to have a new strength and determination they hadn't seen in her before.

No longer thinking or talking negatively, Melody asked her parents to make a house rule that conversations about her cancer be kept to only about her healing. If anyone mentioned that she was 'sick', she'd put up her hand and correct them, explaining that she was 'healing'. Anything she thought of as negative was forbidden. No scary TV shows were allowed, no sad songs, just happy, positive, upbeat, fun vibes were allowed around her from now on.

Although it was hard at first to turn off the nightly news, Melody's dad quickly got used to it and was mindful of his daughter's new rule replacing the negative with the positive and being as fun and uplifting as possible around her. The rules worked a treat, and soon Melody's laughter once again filled the house, and the happier energy rippled through her family and to their friends too.

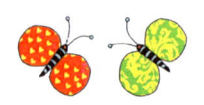

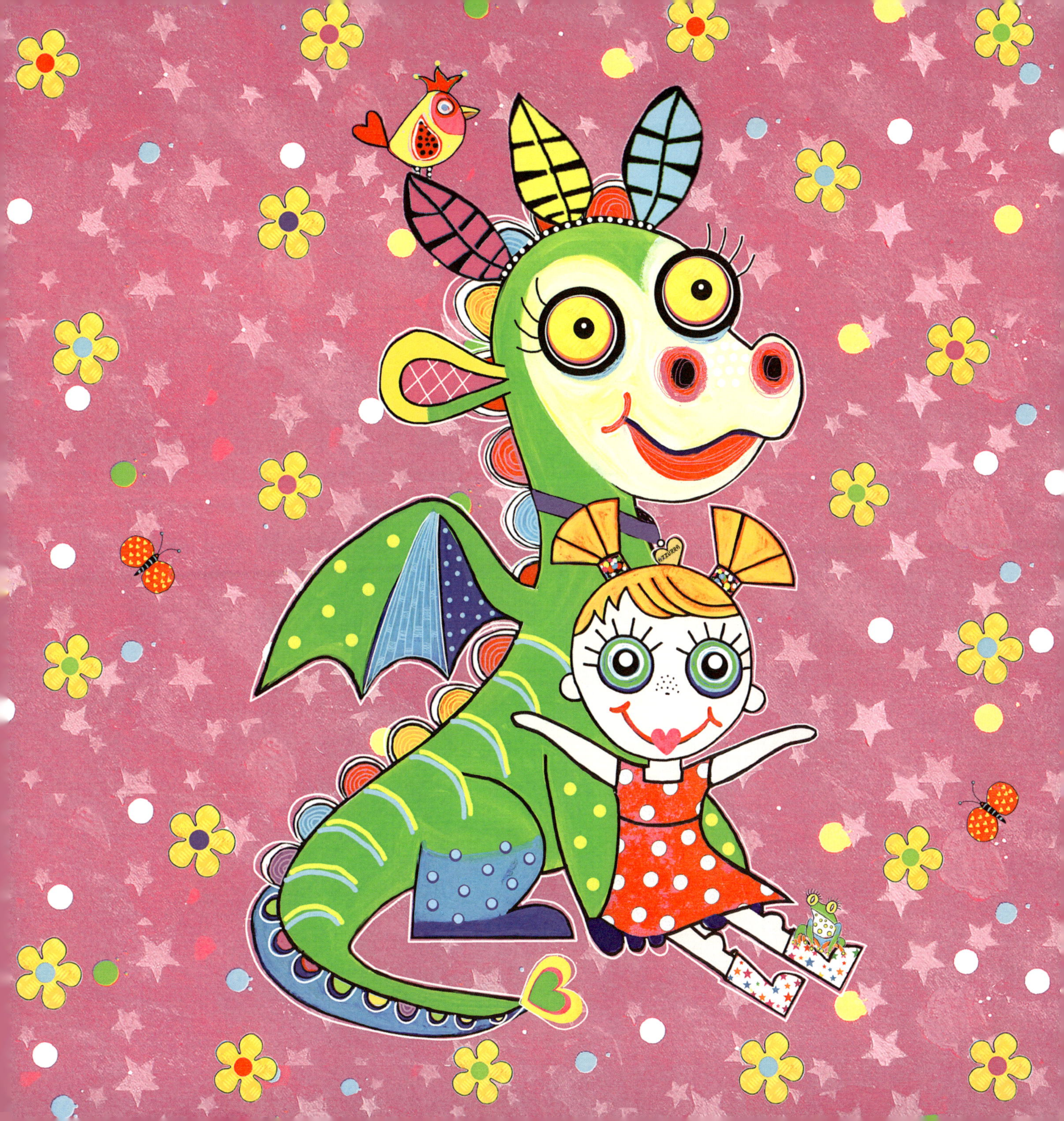

One morning Melody woke up to a cold, icy day. Her curtains remained closed and she felt a chill that no amount of cuddling into her blankets could shake off. Azzurra curled around her to help keep her warm, but Melody couldn't stop shivering.

Her mum covered her with a third blanket as she took her temperature, trying to hide any feelings of worry for her little girl. A check of the temperature gauge showed she had a fever and needed to go to the hospital right away. As the ambulance came nearer to the house, the siren got louder. Melody looked down at Azzurra's worried face.

With tubes in her arm and a tin foil blanket covering her, Melody was wheeled into the cold, white hospital. Concerned faces looked down on her as she tried to force a smile. Instead, a single tear fell down her pale cheek as she gazed about the bleak room. "What was happening?"

Melody felt so unwell—like all the colour was fading out of her. For a minute, she had forgotten all about Azzurra. Feeling sleepy she closed her eyes.

Waking suddenly, Melody heard machines beeping and alarm bells sounding. Doctors and nurses all began talking together in rushed, hurried voices. Panic and fear surrounded Melody but couldn't keep her awake. She drifted in and out of sleep.

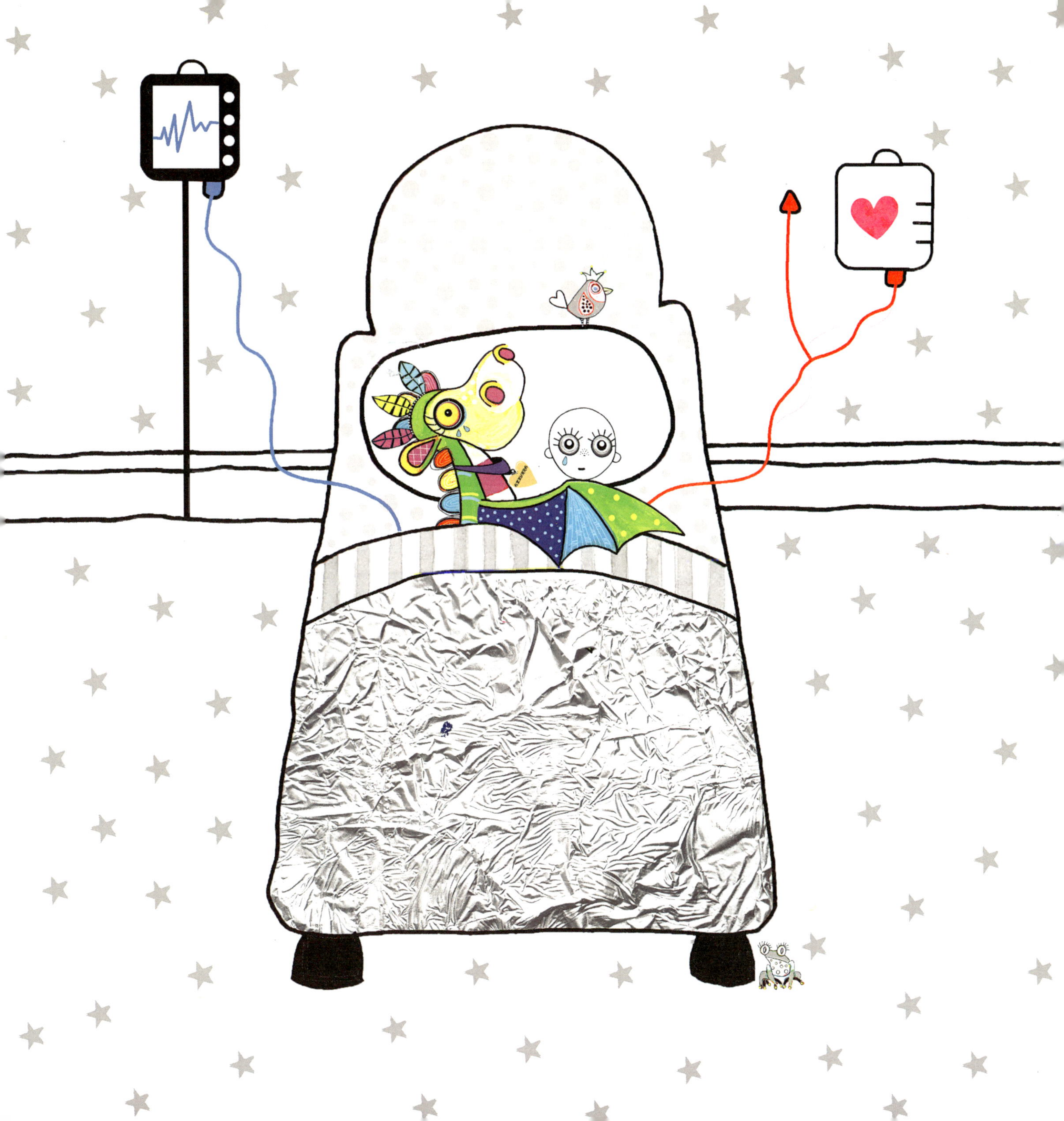

Faintly, she could hear a machine beep like a heartbeat as she slowly opened her eyes. Everything was white. Another machine went 'Whoosh!' and blew air up her nose. A nurse wiped her head and whispered "Shhhhh," as Melody closed her eyes again and drifted back to sleep.

"Beeeeep, whooooosh, ssssshhhhh. Beeeeep, whooooosh, ssssshhhhh." The sounds lulled Melody in and out of a restless sleep. She longed for Azzurra's voice but couldn't hear her anymore. "Had her dragon flown away? Where was Azzurra?" she wondered in the moments she had woken.

And then, as fear began to set in again, Melody felt like she'd been lifted up and off the ground. Higher and higher she went. Up through the white ceiling, up above the hospital roof, and up into the bright blue sky. The sun shone brightly through the clouds and in front of her was the most vivid rainbow she'd ever seen.

Melody was flying straight towards it, but how? As she dared to look down, she saw she was being lifted and flown higher and higher by Azzurra! Her dragon had returned, and she knew exactly what Melody needed.

Melody's happiness soared as they shot across the sky like a sunbeam. "We're together again," Melody whispered, beginning to feel her strength return. She sat up high between Azzurra's wings as they entered the rainbow. She felt each of the colours of the rainbow wash over them.

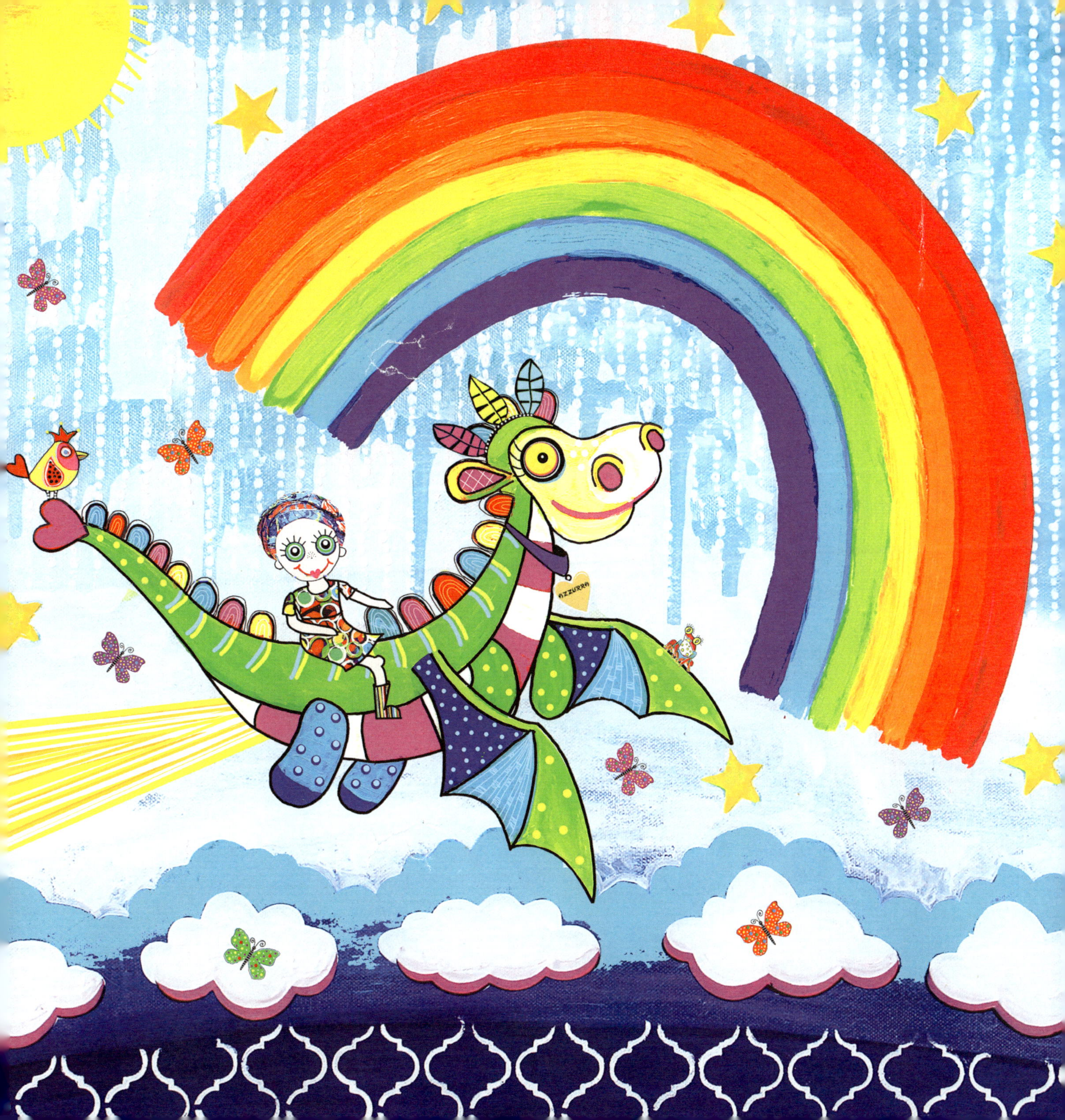
AZZURRA

The colour red felt warm and familiar. It felt like mum and dad's hugs and Nanny Penny's kisses. The feeling of love flooded Melody's body as they flew further through the rainbow.

Then as they left red, and moved into orange, she felt like she'd been given a vitamin C tablet. The kind that made her tongue tingle and tasted like an orange lolly. Her body felt strong and her mind became determined again.

Happiness filled her heart as Azzurra carried her into yellow. Bright happy yellow, like laughter on a summers' day.

The colours of this rainbow seemed to have magical powers.

Blue made her feel calm and clear, green made her feel safe and healthy, and indigo made her feel wise. Melody felt every bit of her body and mind being somehow healed as they flew through each colour.

It was the colour violet, however, that had the most impact on her. Once Azzurra flew into this magical purple light, Melody sensed her future. She felt all of her dreams were rushing to meet her at that moment, and then—with a flash and a whoosh, Melody was back in her hospital bed.

Bells sounded and beeps grew more insistent as doctors and nurses rushed in. Melody sat up straight in bed and her dad gasped as he held her right hand. She was back and she'd never felt so good!

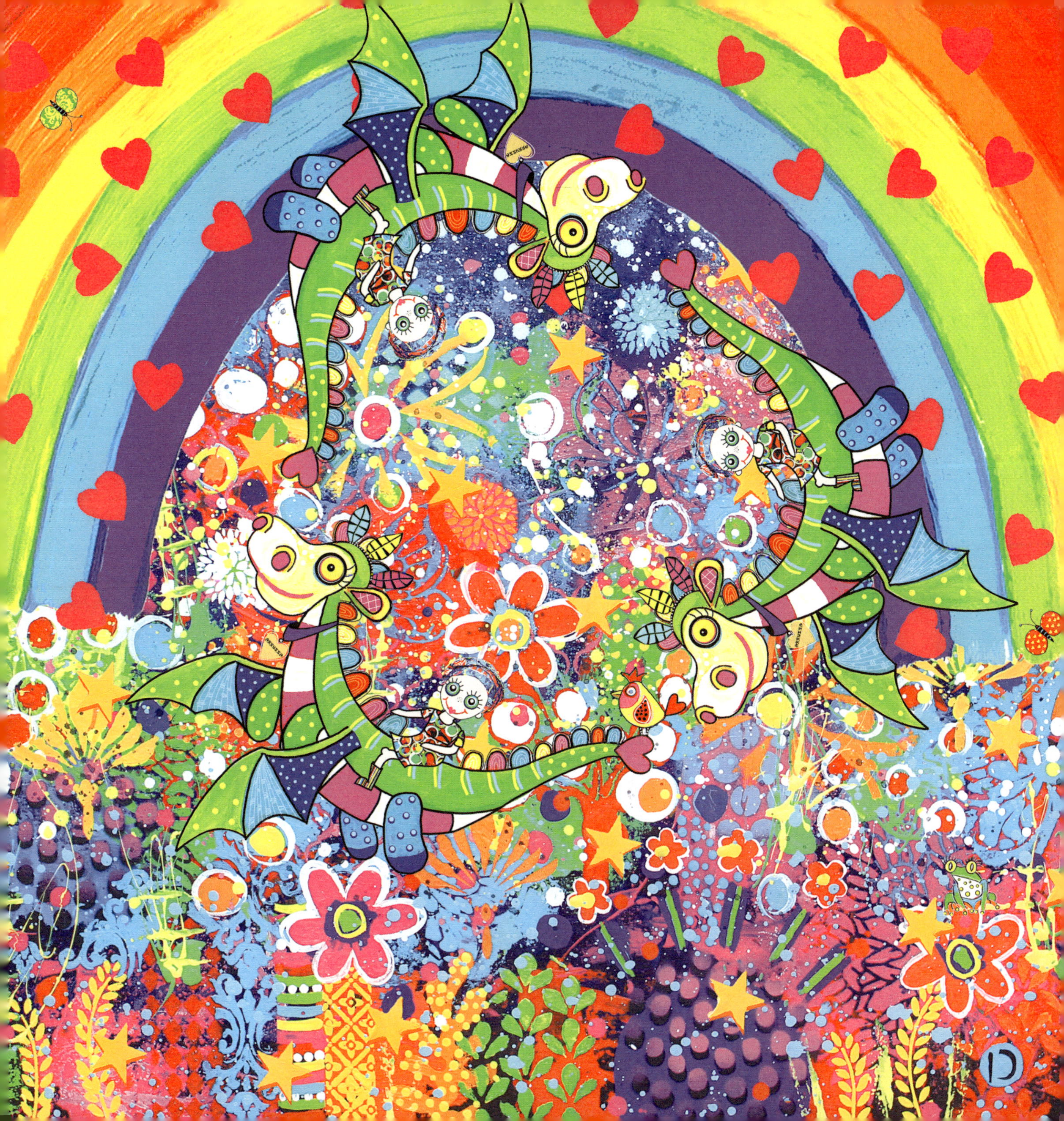

Once again at home and fully recovered, Melody's laughter echoed down the hallway of her home. Auntie Millie had agreed to help paint the girl's room in all the colours of the rainbow. Azzurra loved the idea, as she had watched Melody grow stronger and stronger each day after their trip through the colours of the rainbow.

With Azzura's help, Melody was able to stop her treatments. Her doctors were amazed at how well she was doing. They couldn't explain it but encouraged Melody to keep doing whatever she was doing, as it was working! Melody's future had become so much brighter than she could have ever imagined.

For the first time in months, Melody had hair again! She tied a blue bow in her new, short hair and felt a rush of excitement—today was a special day! Auntie Millie had promised to finish the violet wall behind her bed today. Melody would have loved to stay and help, but today she was finally going to go to school! The house was buzzing with energy. Lunches were being stuffed into back packs, and shoelaces hurriedly tied.

Melody skipped so fast she nearly missed her mum's kiss goodbye. With a squishy hug and a race with her brother to the gate, Melody boarded the school bus. Sitting in the first seat was Bree, her best friend, with a seat saved especially for her. Melody was finally going to school, and with Bree!

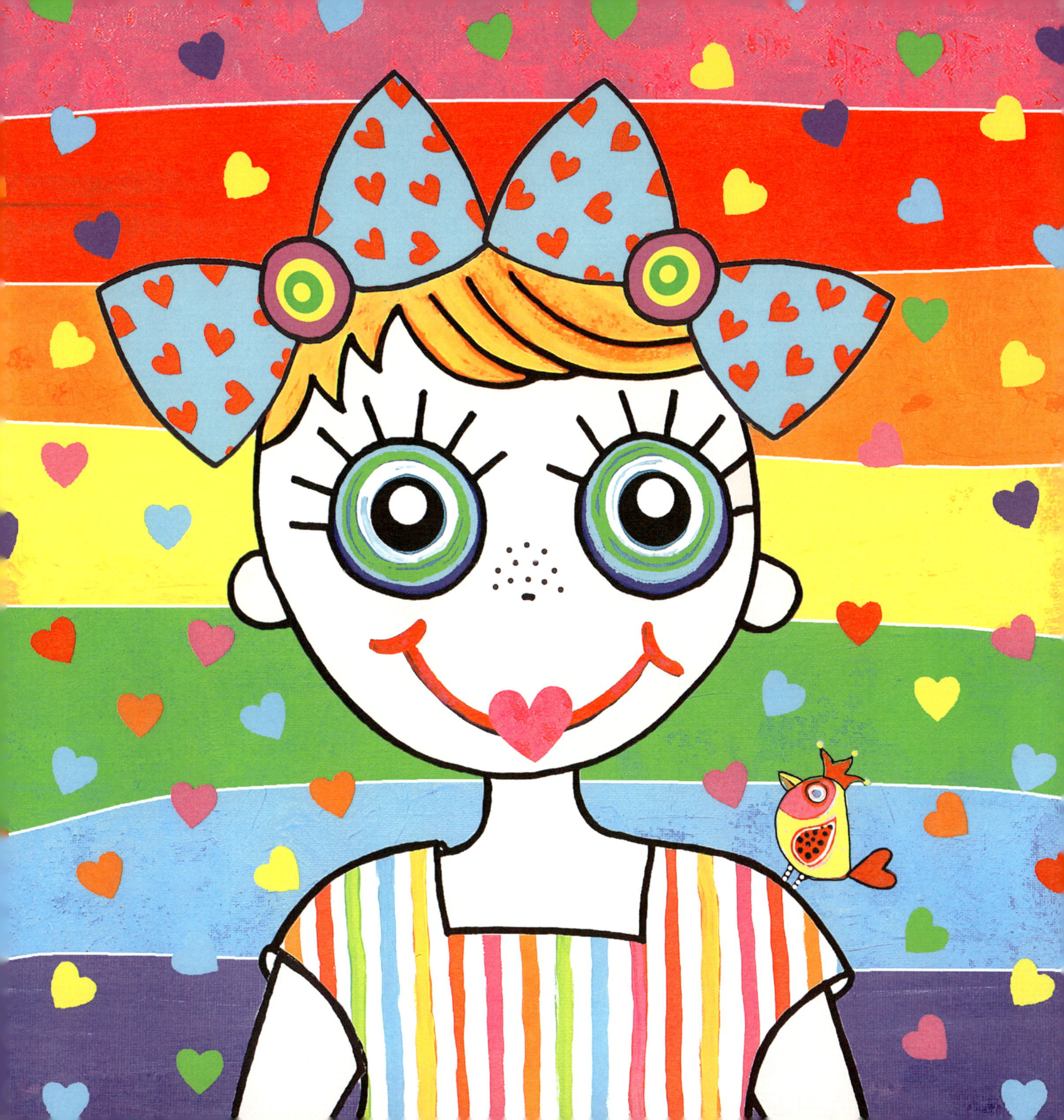

As Melody waved goodbye to her parents and the bus pulled away from the curb she started to feel nervous. "How would she cope with school? Had she been away too long? Would the other kids like her?" she wondered. With her fears beginning to swirl around in her head, she heard the familiar voice of the local bully over her shoulder.

"Sick-girl germs, no returns," spat Tommy, like poison pills of doubt. The bus went quiet. Tommy's words spilled over her like shock waves. "How could he say that? How could he be so mean?" Melody slowly stood up and turned around to face her bully. "Tommy, I'm not sick anymore. I've been healed by my magical dragon!" Melody exclaimed. Tommy's mouth was wide open. "Y-you have a WHAT?" he asked.

Then, out of the corner of her eye, she saw a flash of green. Then a stripe of yellow and blue, followed by a puff of smoke. Was she seeing things? Was Azzurra here on the bus with her? Tommy's voice faded off into the distance as she focused on trying to see where Azzurra was hiding.

The bumpy ride became smooth, and Melody leant over to look out of the window, searching for Azzurra, she knew she was here somewhere, she could feel her. Then Melody spotted her—there she was! Her magnificent wings stretched out, the bus resting on her strong back, gliding along just above the rocky road.

Melody smiled feeling safe again, her fears vanished as she knew then and there that she would never be alone again—Azzurra would be with her forever. Melody knew that life got bumpy sometimes, sometimes real bumpy. But she also knew that her family and her dragon would be there to help lift her up and carry her through the rocky spots to safety.

As Melody's bus arrived at school, she smiled knowingly. She knew she had nothing to worry about as she leaped out of the bus excitedly and ran into school.

After all, she had a magical dragon.

She had Azzurra.

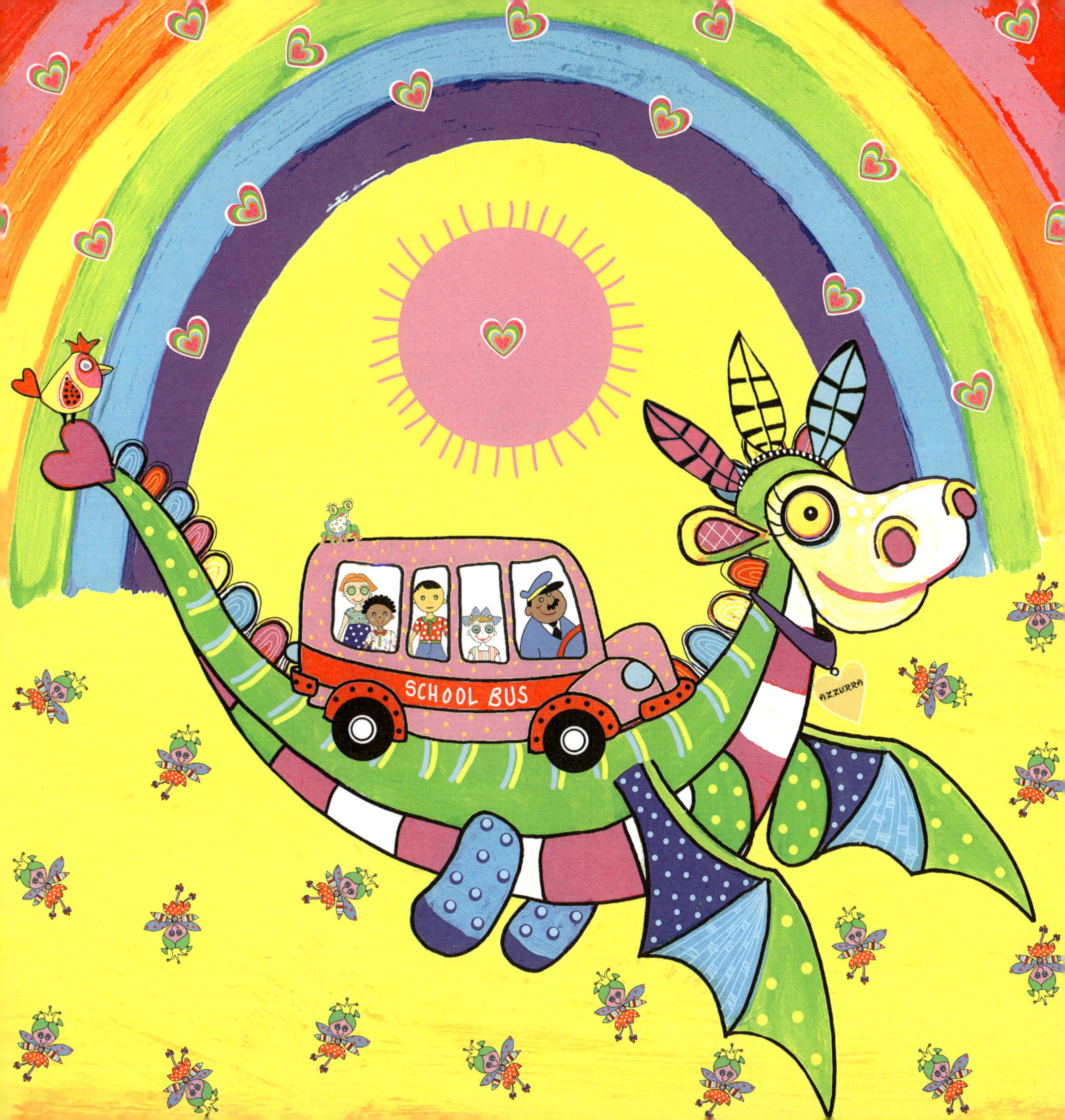
SCHOOL BUS
AZZURRA

How many fairies can you find?

"Look out for the next books in The Dragons of Plenshia Series, with the adventures of Azzurra's siblings Luka and Asher to come"

To Contact Mel :

Facebook: https://www.facebook.com/Dragons.Plenshia

Instagram: @meldeedzelde | @dragons.plenshia

Mel Dee Dzelde is a qualified teacher having achieved her Bachelor of Education majoring in Drama and English. She decided early on in her career that working in the media was far more suitable, and went on to become an ACRA-nominated Radio Announcer and Content Director.

Mel has three adult sons, three Cavalier King Charles Spaniels, a cat, some birds and a Husband who loves movies.

When Mel was pregnant with her third son, she was diagnosed with a liver tumor the size of a golf ball. She recovered fully from that initial cancer scare only to have to face Stage Four Cancer three more times.

Now, after beating cancer multiple times, Mel has been diagnosed with MND/ALS.

Mel is currently a Cancer Survivor and a Motor Neurone Disease Thriver, and she uses her own "Inner Dragon" to give her the strength to fight both diseases.

She can be found on Facebook and Instagram.

To Contact Donna:

Website: www.donnasharam.com

Facebook: www.facebook.com/DonnaSharamArt

Instagram :@donnasharamartgallery

Donna Sharam is an Australian based artist and designer. Collaborations with leading Australian and International brands sees her joyful art and products in homes from Singapore to Miami to Byron Bay near her home and studio.

Donna studied at Sydney College of the Arts and started painting full-time in the early 2000's. Her art mantra is colour, joy and imagination, her zest for life is reflected in her art and is true to her heart.

Donna says, "As for my painting, I think the brush merely tints the canvas: it is imagination that produces art. I have always been drawn to the quirky and different. 'Normal' is not a word I use. My work owes nothing to tradition: I paint with joy and passion and my art is for everyone".

Donna calls her art 'Smile Style' and her hope is that her art brings joy and happiness to all who view it. Find her on Facebook, Instagram and visit her website to see more art @ www.donnasharam.com